Quality Education and Training for the Adult Unemployed

A Manual for Planners and Managers in Further Education

Further Education Unit

ISBN 1 85338 278 7

Copyright © 1992 Further Education Unit
Copyright © 1992 National Institute of Adult Continuing Education

FEU registered charity no. 326347

CONTENTS

section 1

THE CONTEXT

Planning for a changing labour market

The education and training context

Who are the unemployed?

Section 1
THE CONTEXT

This manual is designed to support college management teams in the planning and delivery of effective learning opportunities for unemployed people, within the context of changes in the economy, labour market, education and training policy. It builds upon past and present recommendations of both the FEU and NIACE REPLAN programmes.

PLANNING FOR A CHANGING LABOUR MARKET

The Challenge

Colleges will need to ensure that plans for the unemployed not only take into account major trends and likely future developments, but are also flexible enough to be effective when the direction or speed of change turns out to be different from what was originally predicted.

Numerous reports on the national labour market and skill trends have highlighted several key issues for the British economy in the 1990s. These are:

International developments and competition

The impact of the SEM (Single European Market) will probably be one of the most immediate issues for the early 1990s – and likely effects may well include rationalisation of enterprise and industry on a Euro-wide scale, an increase in the mobility of labour, particularly at higher skill levels, and increased competition for British companies. Other influences are likely to be the development of new markets in Eastern Europe and an increase in competition from the 'Pacific Rim' countries.

New technologies and materials

These will continue to have an impact on the economy and labour market, particularly in terms of the application of information technology, developments in the potential of new materials and biotechnology.

Environmental concerns and pressures

It is clear that these have increasingly important implications for the skills of the future.

Population and labour force changes

According to *Labour Market Skill Trends 1991/2* the following key changes will occur:

- By 1994 there will be 1 million fewer 16–19-year-olds than in 1984.
- The labour force is expected to grow by 800,000 by the year 2001.
- The average age of the labour force will also be higher and most of the increase, over 95%, will be accounted for by women.

New skill requirements

To meet these challenges a different range of skills will emerge:

- Higher-level skills overall – more technicians, fewer operatives, more managers, fewer supervisors, more professionals.
- Specialist skills in new or growing areas of work to implement new technology (correspondingly fewer in shrinking areas of work).
- Regular updating and upgrading within occupations (we face qualitative as well as quantitative skills shortages)
- Training for increased job flexibility (e.g. enabling operators to programme machines, or undertake jobs covering several related skills).
- Wider management appreciation of the implications of new technologies and techniques – especially the organisational implications.
- A much stronger base of general competences at all levels in the workforce.
- Increasing enterprise and initiative across the workforce.

See Appendix 1 for more detailed national information.

Key issues for college planners

How can the college prepare for the likely future developments while at the same time meeting immediate demands?

How can flexibility be built into education or training so that programmes can adapt quickly to changes?

How far is your local labour market or occupational profile following national or regional trends?

Which groups are under-represented in your labour market at present?

To what extent do the skills of the unemployed match local skills shortages?

What national economic developments are likely to have a major impact on your local area?

What are the most important local or sector recruitment difficulties?

What are the main causes of these difficulties?

Which sectors in your labour market are likely to be most affected by increased international and European competition?

THE EDUCATION AND TRAINING CONTEXT

The Challenge

The need to widen access to learning, assessment and accreditation has become a nationally recognised imperative in order to meet the challenges outlined in the previous paragraphs. Recent initiatives in education and training reflect the need for a flexible approach to learning and the need to increase achievement levels, by encouraging and motivating people to be responsible for their own learning, and for the assessment and accreditation of their competence, whether in paid or unpaid work.

The White Paper *Employment for the 1990s* (Cm 540, 1989) placed emphasis on assessing and meeting training needs at a local level, by giving local employers considerable responsibility and involvement in vocational education and training through the creation of Training and Enterprise Councils (TECs) and Local Enterprise Companies (LECs). In aiming to achieve this strategic purpose, TECs and LECs have been given specific responsibility for planning and administering public investment in work-related education and training, by identifying priorities and commissioning appropriate training and related services to meet local labour needs. In November 1991, *A Strategy for Skills, 1992–93*, a guidance framework on helping TECs/LECs to forward their corporate and business plans (see Appendix 2, A), outlined the need to work towards six priorities:

> '*to ensure that all our people, including those who need particular help because they are at a disadvantage in the job market, have the opportunity to fulfil their potential.*'

In particular, Priority 4 focuses on 'people who are unemployed and those at a disadvantage in the jobs market must be helped to get back to work and to develop their abilities to the full' (Appendix 2, C outlines the ways in which this can be implemented).

Running through all the priorities is the steer towards world class targets and life-long learning (see Appendix 2, B). Increasingly, TECs are being encouraged to require outputs from their training providers in the form of achieved NVQs, and sub-NVQs such as Word and Number Power. This trend has major implications for the cost-effective planning and provision of opportunities for unemployed people. A further constraint, caused by the recession and increases in unemployment, has meant that TEC funding from the Department of Employment for training unemployed adults has not been increased in real terms, and so has tended to be redirected to Aim and Guarantee groups only (see Appendix 2, D).

The changes to Further Education proposed by the White Paper *Education and Training for the 21st Century* (Cm 1536, 1991) are also intended to improve access to participation and increase levels of achievement. It seems likely that funding from the Further Education Funding Council will offer incentives to expand participation by direct funding related to student numbers, and will aim to boost achievement by means of differential weightings for higher level NVQs. Funding for adults from the Council will be focused upon provision which:

- leads to academic or vocational qualifications
- provides access to higher education, or to higher levels of further education
- enables learners to acquire basic skills, or skills in English for speakers of other languages
- caters for adults with special educational needs
- in Wales, enables adults to learn or improve their ability to speak Welsh.

It would appear that if both TECs and further education colleges are to provide realistic, flexible learning opportunities for the unemployed and also achieve hard outputs and adequacy of funding, then they will need to take full account of each others' strengths and resources, and plan a partnership approach to meeting the local needs of unemployed adults.

Key issues for college planners

How can the college prepare for the delivery and achievement of world class targets?

How can equitable provision for the unemployed be planned against a background of what will always be limited funding?

How can the TEC/LEC, college and other agencies best meet the realistic training needs of unemployed adults in their area?

What planning mechanisms can be established between the TEC/LEC, college and employment service to make the best possible use of available resources?

What resourcing/planning mechanisms can be established to meet both the individual needs of the unemployed and the growing need to accredit the outcomes of training – which may also become increasingly important to funding?

What opportunities can be made available to encourage TECs/LECs/colleges/Employment Services in an area or region to meet and share their concerns about work with the adult unemployed?

WHO ARE THE UNEMPLOYED?

The Challenge

College planners are faced with the challenge of developing opportunities for the unemployed, when the definition of 'unemployed' covers an extremely diverse and complex range of interpretations, characteristics and individual education and training needs. Perhaps the only single common characteristic is that unemployed people do not have full-time paid jobs, which implies, but does not prescribe, that they have 'time', and reduced or minimal financial status. Further presumptions about the status of 'unemployed' may make the planning of opportunities quite inappropriate or irrelevant for many potential learners.

The diagrams opposite show some of the main sub-groups of unemployed people. The second diagram shows specific sub-groups with special needs.

Colleges, particularly those funded by TECs and Employment Services, will need to know the Employment Service criteria for eligibility as unemployed person:

(a) An individual signing on with the Employment Service and regarded by the Employment Service as being available for work; or

(b) A person receiving Ivalidity Benefit, Sickness Benefit or Severe Disablement Allowance; or

(c) The dependant of someone who satisfies (a) or (b) above, for whom a dependant's allowance is paid, i.e. people not in receipt of direct benefits;

(d) The dependants of a benefit recipient who has entered Training for Adults, subject to the dependant being unemployed for 26 weeks.

(See also Appendix 3 for requirements for the 26-week unemployment qualifying period.)

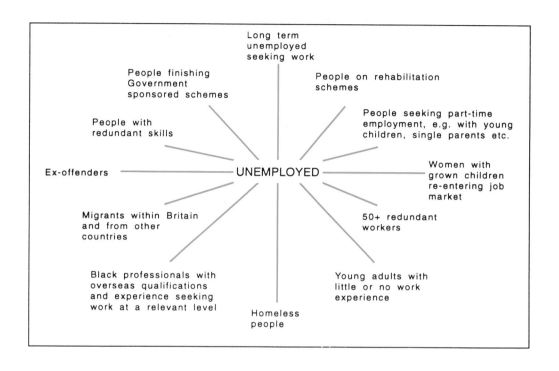

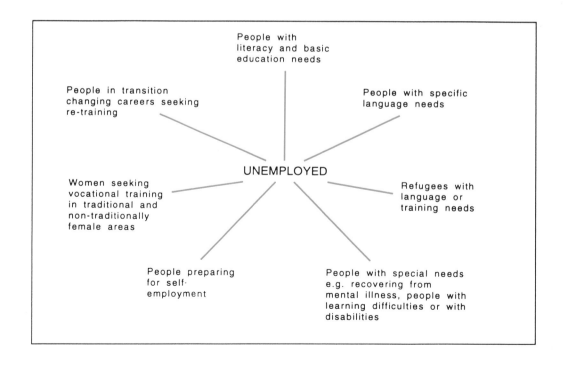

Key issues for college planners

Does the college carry out regular training audits of the diverse community it serves in planning education and training priorities?

How does the college ensure that the personal development and training needs of potential and actual unemployed learners are identified and provided for?

Does the college have good relationships and effective liaison arrangements with the local Employment Service?

Do college staff, particularly those involved with Adult Training, Counselling and Client Services, have a comprehensive and up-to-date knowledge of Employment Service criteria for 'unemployed status' and benefit regulations?

What mechanisms can the college develop to encourage and enhance greater liaison with Employment Service agencies, the TEC/LEC and other providers of training for the unemployed?

What approaches can the college, in partnership with others, develop to increase the awareness of the advantages of learning for unemployed people?

How can the college influence the key funders and sponsors of education and training for the adult unemployed in ensuring that the diversity of individual learning needs are best met to the advantage of all partners concerned?

2 STRATEGIC PLANNING

The planning process

Collaboration and networking

Section 2
STRATEGIC PLANNING

The Challenge

The challenge for colleges in planning provision for the unemployed is the management of potential conflict between:

- short- and long-term planning
- college, local authority and TEC plans
- local and national policy
- the needs of individuals and the demands of the local labour market
- skills shortages and recruitment problems
- the learning process and output-related funding
- economic viability and social responsibility
- individual staff training needs and corporate development needs
- profit and loss-making provision.

These are just some of the dilemmas colleges are facing in planning opportunities for unemployed adults, which is why it is so important that planning time-frames with short- and long-term targets are put into operation.

THE PLANNING PROCESS

Any attempt made to resolve some of the dilemmas posed in the introduction to this section should reflect the institution's own **vision** and **mission**. In setting planning aims and objectives the key questions to ask should be:

- does the college prioritise its mission as 'social' or 'economic'?
- does the college serve the needs of the young people in its community or all members of its community regardless of status and background?
- does the college think its purpose is to help people find jobs, or to help them gain qualifications, or to become more self-fulfilled?
- does the college regard learning opportunities for unemployed adults as an entitlement or as a favour?
- is college provision for the unemployed seen as a loss-leader in the short-term, but as an effective marketing strategy in the long-term?
- is provision for the unemployed seen as a low priority, low status activity?
- is there evidence that the college will commit appropriate resourcing to this area of provision?

Many colleges have developed mission statements that highlight key concepts of equality, equity and entitlements to guidance and to life-long learning. TECs have highlighted their commitment to providing for the unemployed through statements such as:

> *'The TEC will unite public and private resources to create a stimulating and forward looking training and enterprise environment in the County. It will assist both organisations and individuals alike to realise their full potential and build an ongoing prosperous future for the whole community ...'*

and:

> *'To encourage economic growth in the County through effective training and enterprise whilst ensuring that everyone has the opportunity to contribute to, and share in, this success ...'*

The challenge for strategic planners is converting the rhetoric into reality, and one approach developed in this manual adopts the following planning process:

- the identification of strategic aims
- the identification of goals
- operationalising the objectives
- action plan and responsibilities and method
- milestones
- monitoring and evaluation mechanisms
- performance targets
- resourcing.

The following diagram demonstrates the planning **process** that may take place, building on the Quality Development Plan that ATO status requires.

Planning for the Adult Unemployed
A Process Chart

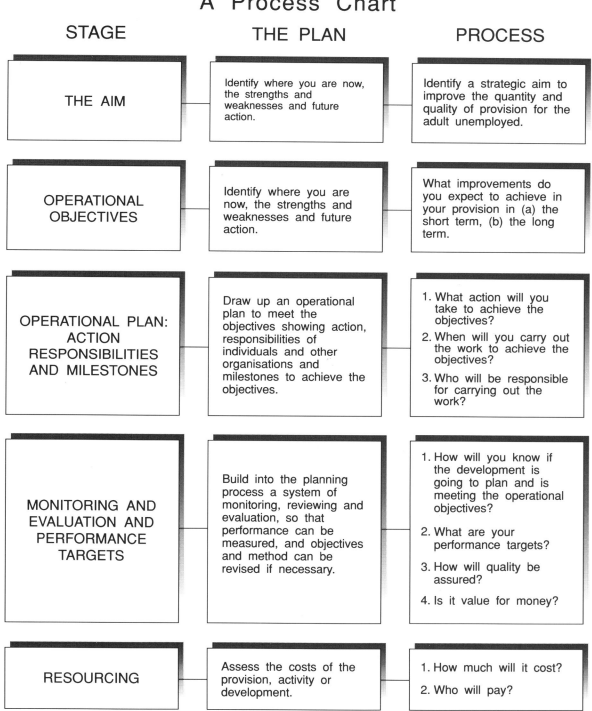

STAGE	THE PLAN	PROCESS
THE AIM	Identify where you are now, the strengths and weaknesses and future action.	Identify a strategic aim to improve the quantity and quality of provision for the adult unemployed.
OPERATIONAL OBJECTIVES	Identify where you are now, the strengths and weaknesses and future action.	What improvements do you expect to achieve in your provision in (a) the short term, (b) the long term.
OPERATIONAL PLAN: ACTION RESPONSIBILITIES AND MILESTONES	Draw up an operational plan to meet the objectives showing action, responsibilities of individuals and other organisations and milestones to achieve the objectives.	1. What action will you take to achieve the objectives? 2. When will you carry out the work to achieve the objectives? 3. Who will be responsible for carrying out the work?
MONITORING AND EVALUATION AND PERFORMANCE TARGETS	Build into the planning process a system of monitoring, reviewing and evaluation, so that performance can be measured, and objectives and method can be revised if necessary.	1. How will you know if the development is going to plan and is meeting the operational objectives? 2. What are your performance targets? 3. How will quality be assured? 4. Is it value for money?
RESOURCING	Assess the costs of the provision, activity or development.	1. How much will it cost? 2. Who will pay?

This process-led approach should enable planners of learning opportunities for the adult unemployed to assess:

- where they are now
- where they want to get to
- who should be involved
- how they can get there
- when they can realistically get there
- what steps have to be taken
- how good practice can be measured
- how much resourcing is needed
- what the benefits are.

An example follows, showing the planning process for a specific aim.

The Planning Process: An Example

Aim: To increase the supply and objectives of potential labour market entrants.

Operational objectives (there may be more than one): To introduce initial training provision to meet the needs of under-represented or disadvantaged labour market entrants.

Action Plan	Responsibility	Milestones
Collaborate with ABE tutors in developing and implementing provision for language development, ESOL, and basic skills.	Adult Education Co-ordinator	April 199-
Establish 'return to work' provision targeted at women without clear vocational aims at present.	Assistant Principal Equal Opportunities	April 199-
Establish 'career change' provision targeted at redundant workers mainly managers and executives over 45 who need 'job-search' skills to re-enter the labour market.	Business Development Officer	September 199-
Establish collaborative compacts with employers and others to research and develop flexible assessment and training solutions to meet the needs of people with disabilities.	Industrial Liaison Officer and Assistant Principal Equal Opportunities.	September 199-

MONITORING AND EVALUATION

- Baseline studies to establish accuracy of targets.
- Customer satisfaction survey.
- Programme team reviews.
- Use of management information system in carrying out a cost-benefit analysis to establish value for money.

RESOURCING

- College Adult Training budget for staff training, administration development and evaluation costs.
- TEC sponsored training for language development and basic skills.
- ESF funding for women-only provision.
- ESF 'HORIZON' for people with disabilities and the long-term unemployed.
- Employment Services funding for 'Career Change' initiative (Job Review Workshops).

PERFORMANCE TARGETS
(by end of year 1)

- At least 20% of women progressing from training to employment.
- At least 5% of people with disabilities progressing from training to employment.
- At least 10% of long-term unemployed progressing from training to employment.
- At least 10% of ethnically diverse groups progressing from training to employment.
- At least 25% of the unemployed client group reaching NVQ level I.
- At least 50% of the 'Career Change' client group progressing to employment or further training.

COLLABORATION AND NETWORKING

This approach to planning is well suited to the establishment of a cross-college team working with the adult unemployed, and encourages a team to make short- and long-term objectives and plan accordingly. The challenge for the college is to know how to deploy all available resources in ways which not only optimise cost-effectiveness but also maximise flexibility of response. Added to this is the requirement to plan the structure and delivery of learning opportunities in terms of the intended outcomes and standards, which are often the contractual requirements of external sponsors of provision for the unemployed. In this situation some of the key concerns for the college may well be:

- maintaining support for the individuality of learners against a background of funding for stated outcomes
- integrating on-and-off the job training in a meaningful way for the clients
- meeting the requirements of NVQ standards
- maintaining dialogue with local employers and the TEC
- maintaining dialogue with Employment Services and Unemployment Support agencies.

In resolving these issues, networking and collaboration is essential. Not only are internal cross-college teams useful but representatives from external organisations may also be most valuable and should be invited to become involved in planning opportunities for unemployed adults.

Examples of Networks

Unemployed Advisory Committees or Networks

Many local networks were initiated by REPLAN in developing and promoting learning opportunities, and some colleges have now established, co-ordinated and maintained area networks of unemployment specialists who are able to identify gaps in the present provision, and suggest possible ways forward. They can also provide a useful evaluating function in considering the 'college plan' in all its stages of development.

Employment Training Liaison Groups

In some parts of the country these liaison groups were initially established to ensure that the key players in planning and providing ET (for example the local Employment Services, Training Agents, Training Managers and sub-contractors of training) could meet to ensure that channels of communication were kept open. In areas where ET no longer exists in name, these groups of key players often still meet to ensure that the quality of adult training is maintained.

Specialist Networks

In some areas networks of contacts with specialists have been established, often with the support of REPLAN to address issues such as:

- people with disabilities
- the rural dimension

- provision for women
- labour market intelligence systems
- training information and guidance.

Community Group Networks

Colleges that have made valuable links with voluntary sector organisations in the community find that this kind of networking is helpful on several fronts:

- it enables outreach marketing to be more clearly targeted and thus more effective
- the location of outreach provision is more carefully researched, planned and consequently supported
- there is a gradual build up of trust and support for the college by members of the network, who may then act as informal advocates and referral contacts for the college
- the identification of new areas of education and training can emerge from requests for advice from community representatives.

The value of networking and inter-agency partnerships should not be underestimated when planning for the adult unemployed. In *Adult Unemployment and the Curriculum* (FEU, 1985), Watts and Knasel identified three levels of collaboration:

Communication – Where agencies and institutions retain their individual programmes and modes of work, but efforts are made to arrive at a better understanding of each other.

Co-operation – Where institutions and agencies collaborate on a joint project or programme of learning.

Co-ordination – Where institutions and agencies alter their established working patterns to provide an integrated programme.

In practical terms collaboration can help a college to:

- reduce duplication of effort
- improve communication and information channels
- increase inter-agency referrals
- increase knowledge, skills and ideas
- promote advocacy on behalf of unemployed adults
- reduce development costs
- promote quality
- improve the planning process.

section 3

MARKETING

The supply side: people and jobs

The demand side: jobs and people

Market research

Outreach

Publicity and promotion

Inter-agency partnerships

Section 3
MARKETING

The Challenge

The challenge of increasing the overall take-up of appropriate learning opportunities with successful outcomes for unemployed adults implies that colleges will need to identify:

- the learning needs and preferred learning styles of the unemployed
- local skills-shortages and recruitment problems

and to provide

- flexible learning opportunities to meet the needs of the target group
- appropriate training to meet the skills requirements or recruitment shortages of employers.

This challenge of reconciling the needs of individuals and industry should become the focus of a college's marketing strategy in planning and providing education and training for unemployed adults. In this context, a strategy can be best described as the ways in which a college can:

- identify specific market segments and individual learning requirements
- promote a mixed range of learning opportunities built around the needs of individual learners or sponsors of training
- remove barriers to access, achievement and progression by appropriate and relevant promotional activities, such as outreach and publicity
- work with other agencies in reaching the unemployed
- work with other organisations in avoiding gaps or duplication in provision
- carry out an 'effectiveness and satisfaction' survey of existing and past unemployed learners
- develop an 'adult friendly' image through its premises, ethos, language and staff attitudes
- learn from experience and want to carry on learning in developing a quality service for individuals and sponsors alike.

THE SUPPLY SIDE: People and Jobs

The key national trends highlighted in the CBI report *Workforce 2000* are:

A projected long-term decline in the number of young people in the workforce.

A projected increase in the labour force by a million between 1988 and 2000 (it is expected that 90% of this increase will be accounted for by women).

The implication is that since employers can no longer rely on recruiting young people, alternative sources of labour may need to be considered, including:

- the long-term unemployed
- women returners
- ethnic minority groups
- older workers
- people with disabilities.

This changing supply of labour will require changes in recruitment policy and working practices in order to involve non-traditional employees, and this labour-market flexibility will inevitably need a more flexible response to training, particularly for unemployed people or returners to the job market.

However, these general national trends will need to be re-interpreted in a local context which may vary considerably from one Travel to Work Area (TTWA) to another. This kind of local information may well be already available from:

- TEC local labour market information services
- DSS Offices
- Unemployed Workers Centres
- Employment Services/Job Centre
- Educational Guidance Services for Adults.

However, evidence suggests that detailed information on the skills of unemployed people is less well researched and documented than information about skills shortages, and so it may be advisable to carry out a local skills audit or survey as an integral aspect of market research.

THE DEMAND SIDE: Jobs and People

Making accurate forecasts about future employment opportunities is notoriously difficult, particularly as the structure of employment has changed so dramatically in recent years, for example:

- the shift from manufacturing to service sector employment
- rapid expansion in part-time and temporary employment
- rapid expansion of professional and technical jobs at the expense of unskilled, operative-level jobs
- the collapse of traditional job boundaries, replaced by more flexible working patterns, diversified or customised products and new technologies.

The implications for providers of training are significant and colleges will need to know what the local business and economic community is prioritising, and encourage the sharing of information about skill shortages, updating and re-training requirements in order to avoid any mis-match between **labour supply** and **labour demand**.

MARKET RESEARCH

Market research is an essential stage in the planning of learning opportunities, and the information and intelligence gathered needs to be regularly updated, reviewed and fed into existing and planned provision. It should become an integral aspect of all planning and monitoring of education and training for unemployed adults. The key implication of data collection is the establishment of an effective Management Information System, without which the effort spent on research will be wasted.

In this context **market research** may need to be carried out from **three** perspectives at local level:

The Labour Market

- what are the realistic employment opportunities?
- where are they?
- when will they happen – immediately or in the long-term?
- which sector has skill shortages?
- which sector has recruitment problems?
- how can this information be obtained?

The Training Market

- what provision is already available?
- where are the gaps?
- is there any duplication?
- who has the competitive edge?
- how can this information be obtained?

The Unemployed Learners' Market

- where are they?
- who are they?
- what skills do they have?
- what training do they perceive they need?
- do these perceptions meet the needs of the labour market?
- how can help be provided?
- how can this information be obtained?

The Labour Market

A considerable amount of information and intelligence is already available and accessible at a local level:

- local authority Economic Development Units, Planning and Chief Executives' Departments
- TEC advisory and information services
- employer networks such as Chambers of Commerce
- higher education research from departments such as Urban Studies, Economics and Social Sciences
- sector specific employment agencies
- regional DTI offices.

The main challenge for colleges is the interpretation of this information in the light of the specific needs of actual unemployed learners. It will often be more practical to carry out a customised sector- or employer-specific audit of skills requirements and perceived training needs. This could then lead to the development of customised training or Adult Compact arrangements.

A variety of research techniques can be used, each with its own strengths, but each with its own costs. The most commonly used methods include:

- postal (reply paid) questionnaires either direct to individual employers or indirectly through employer organisations, meetings, mailings or publications
- personal interviews by telephone or face to face
- promotional or media campaigns
- link with national promotional events.

With limited resources, it may be necessary to consider the benefits of collaborative market research, for example with:

- polytechnic or university departments, where these institutions offer the staff and graduate researchers, and colleges provide 'the problem' and administrative support
- TEC development funding
- DTI regional offices colleges provide the staffing, DTI provides the backing
- European Information and Advice Centres: the Centres provide the data, colleges interpret it and place it context
- Chamber of Commerce support: Chambers distribute questionnaires, colleges provide an analysis for use by both parties.

The Training Market

To avoid duplication of effort or the missing of potential markets, it may be useful to carry out an audit of local providers of education and training for unemployed adults in the private, voluntary and statutory sectors, in order to identify:

- geographical gaps in provision
- potential collaborative partners
- effectiveness of your pricing policy
- new venues for delivery

- additional learner support structures, such as unemployed centres, guidance services, childcare provision
- opportunities for new development and promotional activities
- evidence for withdrawing, reducing or expanding certain provision.

In certain areas the REPLAN initiative, mainly through Education Support Grant funded officers, has resulted in the development of directories or databases of information about potential learning opportunities for unemployed adults. An extensive audit may not be necessary, therefore. However, where this REPLAN information does not exist or may be out of date, it could be helpful to make contact with:

- the local authority or independent guidance services for adults
- TEC Advisory Services or Gateway Centres
- TAP (Training Access Points), if separate from the above
- local adult learning/access networks
- Community Education Service of the local authority
- Rural Community Council for information on local village appraisals
- Community Relations Officers and black community support groups
- Council for Voluntary Services
- Unemployed Workers' Centre
- Council for the Disabled
- the regional SKILL agent.

If, after this initial search, the information is dated or limited, it may be useful to carry out a more extensive 'training market' research exercise. Some colleges have recognised the value of knowing who else is operating in their area, and have instigated the setting up of inter-agency networks.

Other colleges have involved existing students, perhaps undertaking social sciences or community oriented learning opportunities, in 'finding out' what is happening in the area they live in. The research not only supports the students in their study, but provides a cost-effective marketing mechanism.

All of this data may be used to inform the college planning cycle and shape college development.

The Learners' Market

This aspect of market research is probably the least well-developed, yet evidence suggests that surveys of potential, existing and past learners as well as sponsors of learners can be one of the most valuable forward planning tools. In some colleges a student survey is an integral aspect of all provision, and has become a natural rather than a contrived feature of learning programmes. If the process is to be effective then all staff need to be involved and this, at least initially, will have staff development and resourcing implications. Evidence suggests, however, that once the infrastructure is established the benefits will far outweigh the disadvantages in staff time and cost.

Researching the Potential Market

Much of the early REPLAN research established that personal contact investigating the learning needs of unemployed people was the most effective way of responding to the potential market.

In *Listening To You ... Listening To Us* (FEU, 1987) a systematic approach to market research was advanced which involved:

- an analysis of the statistical profile data for the area
- mapping a street poll
- 'door knocking' interviews.

A point worth noting was that unemployed people themselves were involved in the design and review of the questionnaire to be used, which resulted in much more effective data collection. Similarly, a NIACE REPLAN project (1988) further extended the involvement of the potential learner by encouraging local unemployed people to carry out the research. As one of the volunteer workers at the Owton Fens local Learning Centre in Hartlepool said:

'Because the workers are local residents, they are more sensitive and aware of the problems people who live on the estate face ... it's because they are local and have been in the same situation.'

Hartlepool College certainly found the information most influential in formulating its plans for adult training and being more responsive to the community it served.

Researching the Existing Market

As part of a college programme and quality assurance procedure, it is essential to consider and act upon the satisfaction ratings and recommendations for the improvement of provision made by existing clients and sponsors. Some organisers of provision encourage feedback after each learning session, others favour more formal procedures midway, during and at the end of a course or event. The most favoured ways of collecting this kind of information for reporting purposes include:

- group discussion and oral, written or video-taped feedback
- individual interviews
- completion of questionnaires
- computer-aided self-analysis
- the use of a 'critical friend' or external evaluator.

Many colleges have developed sophisticated approaches to the collection, collation and use of the data as part of the development of course review systems and their 'quest for quality'. Similarly, many TECs, in their roles as contractors of training for the unemployed, are specifying the need for ongoing quality control and review.

A recent example of a collaborative approach to marketing funded by Norfolk and Waveney TEC and Norwich City Council was carried out by a team from Norwich City College who set out to:

- identify financial barriers which might have been impeding the skilling/reskilling of the local Norwich/Norfolk workforce

- generate proposals for both policy and practical initiatives which could assist financially disadvantaged groups of adults to enter into vocational training
- stimulate training of a relevantly skilled workforce to meet local labour demands.

The report (De Bell, D. and Davies, B. *Paying for Skills: Financial barriers to access to vocational training for adults*, Norwich City Council, 1991) based on 300 interviews with past and present clients at the college, made a number of recommendations which should be considered by all planners and providers of education and training in the area.

Researching Past Clients

In *Supporting Unemployed Adults in FE* (FEU, 1989) an extensive survey of past clients, including those who had left early from a course, demonstrated that a college experience, in this case Stockton-Billingham in Cleveland, had been a positive one for the majority of people included. It also highlighted the fact that people tend to 'drop out' within the first six weeks of a learning opportunity, suggesting that perhaps provision should be based on shorter modular time frames supported by more frequent enrolment patterns, a suggestion that was later adopted by the college in aiming to be more flexible.

This 'tracking' of past students not only influences present college policy and practice, it is also one of the most cost-effective marketing practices in attracting new students. For example:

- it can demonstrate that the college is a caring and professional organisation which stimulates re-enrolments
- 'good news stories' and customer references are a useful way of promoting the college through the media
- contact with ex-customers may lead to the identification of new training needs and new learning opportunities.

The potential benefits of this kind of research activity are unlimited as long as there is the capacity to collect, collate and process the data through the college management information system, linked to the college and area development planning structures.

OUTREACH

The REPLAN programme established the appropriateness of outreach through many of its research and development projects, and the term has become increasingly popular, even though it may be used in different contexts to mean very different things (see *Drawing on Experience*, FEU/NIACE, 1990).

Organising courses in local community premises beyond the main campus of the parent institution.

Persuading other agencies to promote, publicise and recruit for one's own courses.

Negotiating with other community-based organisations to act as providing agencies.

Supporting the efforts and programmes of other independent local organisations.

Facilitating the development of self-help learning groups.

Making direct contact with members of the identified target group.

Mobilising word-of-mouth networks and peer group effort in publicising provision.

Disseminating information and publicity in new or unusual places.

Quite clearly 'outreach' as a marketing approach attempts to:

- encourage groups and individuals to take greater responsibility for their own learning
- move the college away from its institutional restrictions and bureaucracies, and to develop an open, two-way communication channel with the community it serves
- promote the college as a community resource which reaches out to the diverse populations it serves.

An effective outreach strategy should be organised around the following main considerations:

College aims and objectives

- set out clearly why outreach activities are undertaken and what outcomes are anticipated, stressing that outreach is an integral activity
- link outreach to college market research activities in interpreting actual need and demand
- complement more formal approaches to publicity and promotion such as advertising and leafleting
- continuously evaluate the processes of outreach

Collaboration

- plan with other agencies working with unemployed adults in the area, developing collaborative networks
- carry out community audits to find the best venues for college delivery – for example village halls, pubs, hotels, community centres, libraries, etc.

Staffing and resourcing

- outreach should be co-ordinated by an outreach team or worker

- the skills required in outreach development and delivery should be recognised and valued
- appropriate staff who are, for example, familiar with local neighbourhoods, fluent in mother-tongue languages and empathetic to the needs of the unemployed should be employed
- cost and resource outreach appropriately, perhaps using a 'weighting' formula
- active senior management support and commitment is essential

Meeting learner needs

- encourage progression routes and smooth transition from community-based learning to college-based learning delivery and vice versa
- developments should be community or learner-led rather than college or provision-led.

PUBLICITY AND PROMOTION

Promotional activities, including publicity, are important aspects of the marketing process, particularly to unemployed adults who may well need more specifically targeted information than traditional college users. Research carried out by Cleveland Technical College (FEU, 1989) revealed that inaccurate public perceptions of further education, compounded by inappropriate publicity, was one of the main reasons for low participation by unemployed people. Such views were also frequently expressed by sponsors of training such as TECs. The conclusions to be drawn from this research, therefore, is that effective publicity must:

- reach its intended audience
- persuade this audience that the provision on offer is worth further consideration
- accurately portray the provision as having something useful and worthwhile as an outcome
- use style, images and language with which the unemployed can identify
- highlight information and images that will help overcome barriers to using the college. Examples of positive information might be that:
  - a creche is available
  - 10.00 – 14.00 timing is standard
  - there is access for wheelchairs
  - there is multi-lingual publicity
  - college policy is to use personal contact names for further information
  - information is jargon-free and multi-lingual where appropriate
  - casual publicity gives an idea of the range and flexibility of provision on offer
- make use of informal publicity channels through existing adult clients by encouraging them to promote the value of college learning to friends and relatives
- relate to and be part of the college marketing policy and plan
- be closely evaluated in assessing the effectiveness and appropriateness of different methods.

A variety of promotional matters have been developed by planners and providers of training for the unemployed. Recent evidence suggests that a mixed approach which uses every possibility from cable television and radio to word-of-mouth and personal contact is best. The latter may well be the most effective in terms of targeting specific client groups.

Some of the most frequently used promotional activities include:

- mail shots
- leaflets distributed with a free newspaper
- human interest/good news stories in the press
- newspaper advertisements
- radio phone-in slot or jingle
- market stalls, stalls at shows or conventions
- publicity in shops, clinics, doctors' and dentists' surgeries, pubs, supermarkets
- information desks or publicity in Job Centres, DSS, UBO offices or Unemployed Workers' Centres
- publicity via employers declaring redundancies
- posters and publicity in community centres, religious and cultural centres
- mobile information and guidance service
- open days and evenings, summer schools and family learning weekends
- taster sessions.

One point that is often made by providers is the importance of offering information and open days to staff in referral and support agencies who come in direct contact with the unemployed. These staff can then offer much more informed and practical advice to their clients who may wish to take part in a college activity.

Finally, and perhaps most importantly, the image a college presents to the communities it serves depends not only on the type and style of its publicity, but on the people who represent and work in the college – particularly those who are the first point of contact, who are often non-teaching staff. The implication of this is the establishment of a comprehensive staff development programme which highlights the importance of public relations and staff attitudes to particular groups and individuals within the college.

INTER-AGENCY PARTNERSHIPS

Throughout this and other sections there is an emphasis on the need for co-operative working with other agencies (see Section 2 in particular). This is especially important in the planning of opportunities for unemployed adults, as there are many other agencies who have specific interests in unemployment and unemployed people. For example:

- employers
- trade unions
- TECs and TEED
- Job Centres

- Unemployment Benefit Offices
- Department of Social Security
- Social Services Departments
- Race Relations Employment Advisory Services
- Unemployed Workers' Centres
- voluntary agencies
- Educational Guidance Services for Adults
- adult, community and further education services
- schools.

A collaborative multi-agency marketing approach for the unemployed was developed by Peterlee College in Co. Durham in association with many of the above agencies, by establishing an 'Opportunities Shop' in the town centre. This offered a 'one-stop-shop' approach to guidance and information on employment prospects and advice on coping with unemployment.

The main benefit of networking in this way is the provision of a co-ordinated information service to unemployed people, which avoids confusion, duplication and waste of resources. Consequently, a college marketing strategy needs to emphasise co-operation, collaboration and co-ordination rather than competition.

section 4
CURRICULUM MANAGEMENT

Curriculum planning

Curriculum design and delivery

Curriculum content

Learner support

Learning support

Assessment and accreditation

After-care services

Section 4
CURRICULUM MANAGEMENT

The Challenge

In order to balance the concepts of equity and life-long learning with the need to become economically viable and financially independent institutions, colleges will need to manage the curriculum in such a way that:

- long-term aims balance short-term demands
- national policy is interpreted to meet local socio-economic needs
- the supply of labour meets the demand for labour
- training and retraining begins to reduce the 'skills gap'.

CURRICULUM PLANNING

Colleges which are adopting learner-centred approaches and emphasising the importance of learner-support services are likely to be in a better position to match the needs of individuals with the demands of industry and the economy.

In practical terms this means that curriculum planners must take into account the need to create learning opportunities which encourage individuals to become more skilled, adaptable, flexible and personally fulfilled, together with a need to achieve output-related targets within a specified time frame. This balancing act has become the major challenge for providers of education and training for unemployed adults. The most obvious solution, that of developing flexible learning approaches, is capable of application to all learning programmes in further education which seek to:

- remove the barriers to learning (such as fixed enrolment periods and attendance, specific entry requirements inappropriate learning environments, etc.)
- enable people to take responsibility for and control of their own learning, within a supportive learning infrastructure, by helping individual learners to become adaptable, problem solving and independent and thereby assist in the development of a better trained, better qualified workforce
- increase the effectiveness of learning by making it learner-centred, which involves encouraging learners to find their preferred learning style
- increase access to assessment and accreditation appropriate to individual needs and purposes, in helping all learners to achieve their full potential
- create a college ethos of 'inclusiveness and equality' where no one, learner or member of staff, is marginalised or excluded from learning opportunities or support. The advent of NVQs, independent of courses, defined in terms of

outcomes rather than input, and independent of the characteristics of any particular client group, is becoming the output currency of funding for unemployed people. It is now generally accepted in FE that colleges seeking to provide opportunities for the unemployed must guarantee all students flexible access to learning, assessment and relevant accreditation.

CURRICULUM DESIGN AND DELIVERY

This will need to take into account both adult learner needs and, where appropriate, the sponsor's requirements. Colleges which are able to achieve this will be well placed to offer a **mixed-mode** approach to learning opportunities, so that learners will have access to opportunities to suit their preferred style of learning.

Mixed-mode Provision

This could include:

- learning in a group
- taught classes, demonstrations and lectures
- workshops
- simulations
- distance learning
- work based or work-place learning
- independent study with tutor or work supervisor support
- independent study with peer group support.

Individual Learning Programmes

These are built around the needs and aspirations of the learner and the objectives and required achievement targets of the sponsor. The programme emphasis is on active learning rather than teaching, which is supported by an induction or orientation phase, target-setting, review, assessment, recording of progress and achievement. The provision of additional learning support (e.g. language development, numeracy, ESOL, study skills) can be optional in enabling learners to make maximum progress. Barriers, such as those listed below, that impede achievement and access to learning need to be recognised by providers, and where possible removed:

- physical barriers – lack of transport or poor wheelchair access
- inflexible attendance times
- lack of childcare or elderly dependant support
- cost of equipment, books or clothing
- costs of assessment or accreditation services.

Work-based and Work-Place Learning

This may well be the preferred option of both the learner and the sponsor and increasingly colleges are responding in the following ways:

- providing realistic (simulated) work situations in college

- developing assignments or projects to be undertaken in the workplace or at home
- liaising with workplace supervisors in developing appropriate learning programmes
- providing training, assessment and accreditation in the workplace, community setting or in the home.

Development of Pathways and Progression Routes

Unemployed learners may need to enter, leave and re-enter learning programmes more frequently than other adult learners as a consequence of the transitory nature of their status. Colleges therefore need to design and deliver provision in ways that will increase the availability of multiple pathways leading to a variety of qualifications. For example:

- a modular or unitised curriculum based on competences, learning outcomes or learning objectives
- unit credits to be built up over time
- roll-on/roll-off access to units or modules, with the appropriate guidance and support
- open learning assignments should also be available to complement tutor-led approaches so that the learner could work at home if that was a preferred choice
- resource-based, multi-skills learning workshops equipped with quality learning materials and resources should enable unemployed learners to attend at times to suit their convenience and domestic commitments. Workshops could be serviced by learning resources managers (rather than teachers) and learning support staff, both clerical and technical. Staff could assess needs, agree targets, provide appropriate learning opportunities, monitor and review progress and assess achievement
- Computer Assisted Learning (CAL) is proving popular in certain curriculum areas, such as secretarial and business studies. However, both the hardware and software are expensive, so developments have been slow.

CURRICULUM CONTENT

In the 1980s early REPLAN work on planning provision for the adult unemployed suggested that education could 'attempt to respond to the needs of the unemployed' by providing a structure and a sense of purpose, and by helping them to acquire new skills and knowledge which would then help them:

- to cope better with their existing situation
- to escape unemployment and return to employment
- to use their situation as an opportunity to explore new possibilities.

A conceptual framework for the aims and content of educational programmes was proposed around five main objectives:

> Employability: to help unemployed people to develop knowledge, skills and attitudes which will increase their chances of finding and keeping a job.

> Coping: to help unemployed people to develop knowledge, skills and attitudes which will help them to cope with being unemployed.

> Content: to help unemployed people to understand the extent to which the responsibility for being unemployed lies with society rather than with the individual, and to explore possible forms of social, political and community action related to unemployment.

> Leisure: to help unemployed people to develop knowledge, skills and attitudes which will help them to make good use of their increased 'leisure' time.

> Opportunity Creation: to help unemployed people to develop knowledge, skills and attitudes which will enable them to create their own livelihood (*Adult Unemployment and the Curriculum*, FEU, 1985).

It provided a useful framework for the design of a wide range of initiatives for the unemployed, particularly through the Manpower Services Commission (MSC) Wider Opportunities for Training Programme (WOTP). Subsequent changes in funding led to a more focused concentration on 'Employability' and 'Opportunity Creation' through the development of the Job Training Scheme (JTS), RESTART and the emergence of Job Clubs. More recently, the focus of DE funded provision was on specific job-related skills through ET (Employment Training) and Job Searching Skills (RESTART and Job Clubs). However, some colleges have continued to plan and run more general educational programmes for the unemployed, with support from Task Force Funding, ESF and local authority REPLAN developments.

In 1989 the new Training and Enterprise Councils (TECs) were given the responsibility for managing the ET programme (under Block 2 funding) and there are clear indications that the majority of the TECs are planning new and more flexible ways of offering support to the unemployed.

For example, one TEC is restructuring its adult training programme by developing five distinct services:

> A counselling and guidance service for adults through the establishment of Adult Counselling Advice Centres. Counselling vouchers will also be introduced for use by unemployed people.

> A means of recognising experience and skills that people already have. This past experience can be assessed and accredited to help people move into further training or a job.

> Training to prepare people for the job market – 'Initial Training'. This includes Back to Work, Foundation Training, ESL, Literacy and Numeracy.

> Skills training – which will include jobsearch, work placements, review and assessment, 'on the job' training and Open Learning.

> Training for people with special needs. The services will be provided by a range of providers through a system of output-related funding.

Some TECs are also recognising that if the workforce is to become more adaptable, flexible and equipped to solve problems, then perhaps core skills should be introduced as an integral aspect of adult training and re-training.

In areas of specific skill shortages, customised training and the development of Adult Compacts is being promoted, approaches which are particularly suited to employee status learners.

LEARNER SUPPORT

Why?

Central to effective curriculum management is the recognition of the value of support services for adult learners. Adults returning to any kind of learning activity require a variety of support services, particularly if they have had negative school or apprenticeship experiences, or if there has been a long gap since they were involved in any kind of formal or social group activity. Such negative emotions and lack of confidence are made even worse by the effects of redundancy, long-term unemployment and unpaid work status.

When?

Much of the current work on quality-focused organisations emphasises the importance of a never-ending quest for quality and quality improvement. It is an orientation which is mirrored by the need for effective learner support services at all phases of an adult's involvement with a college and its learning programmes. It may be useful to consider a learner's involvement in a college as a four-phase process, with each phase requiring a different degree or type of support.

- pre-entry
- at entry
- during the learning programme
- after the learning programme.

Pre-entry

This is the phase at which interested learners could become clients. They are likely to be:

- unsure of what opportunities are best for them
- unclear about the hidden costs and problems of returning to learning
- uncertain about whether to take the risk for themselves and their dependants
- unaware of the range of opportunities and support available to them
- influenced by negative school experiences and sometimes false impressions of their real abilities.

Colleges will need to offer information, advice and guidance which may well not lead to an enrolment.

(This is a critical phase for planners and managers of FE, and needs to be considered as part of a total marketing/planning strategy.)

At Entry

At this time many potential clients have decided that a learning programme or course is what they want, or at least what they think they want. They will need to be invited and welcomed to the college, enrolled and introduced to the most appropriate learning programme.

During the Learning Programme

The potential client has now become the actual learner, and whatever the level, style, content and planned outcome of the learning programme, the learner will need support on the best way to learn and study, on progress and where to go next.

After the Learning Programme

At this point the clients have been assessed, accredited and qualified and, it is to be hoped, have also enjoyed the learning process! Support will be needed in planning the next steps in terms of self development and possible progression to higher levels of further education, higher education or into employment. This support may not be needed immediately, but after a few weeks or months, colleges may have to provide a kind of after-care service – again a vital component of an effective marketing strategy.

This series of phases offers FE managers a basis on which to plan, resource and set up an integrated learner support system to ensure that learners get the quality service they have been promised.

Developing an Integrated Learner Support Service

The kinds of support required by unemployed adult learners can be grouped as follows, but such a grouping could well have a different emphasis at different phases of a learning programme.

Educational/Vocational Guidance

Information, advice, guidance and counselling should be offered as an integral aspect of all learning opportunities but may well have a different emphasis at different phases of a learning programme.

Practical Support

Information, guidance and referral systems must be available to offer expert advice on financial and personal matters. Support with transport, childcare, older dependants and physical access must also be planned and resourced.

Learning Support

This includes ways in which adults can be helped to get the most out of a learning programme, and may well include study skills, language support, basic skills assistance, assessment and accreditation of prior learning and achievement, action planning and recording of achievement. Specialist support for people with disabilities is also a priority, and should include facilities such as brailling and signing.

Educational/ Vocational Guidance

Educational/vocational guidance is likely to be needed at the pre-entry and at the final phase of a learning programme, for example:

- when someone is initially considering their learning needs and the options available
- at enrolment time, when decisions are made
- towards the end of a programme, when future opportunities need to be assessed and planned for.

Staff based within the college may well provide this function, but increasingly there has been a move towards the development of local adult guidance services offered by external specialists who should:

- offer neutral guidance independent of the interests of any individual provider
- be professionally staffed by educators trained in guidance work
- operate within the context of a collaborative network of providers and referral agencies
- be capable of fulfilling an effective feedback and advocacy role.

Some TECs are considering offering vouchers to unemployed adults for guidance and counselling, in order to enable them to make the best decision about training opportunities. Others are making educational guidance an integral and important aspect of training packages and programmes. In either case the implications for colleges are significant and include such issues as:

- a corporate policy on providing guidance and counselling at all stages and as an integral, not marginal college service
- providing resources for guidance and induction before enrolment in order to help adults make the right choices
- creating mechanisms for planning and networking with local adult guidance services, and other providers of training for unemployed people
- planning a staff development programme for all staff in educational guidance and counselling.

Practical Support

Just as colleges may wish to take advantage of external agencies for educational and vocational guidance, it may also be more appropriate for external, expert advisory agencies to be involved when offering information, advice and counselling on personal matters such as financial and debt counselling, legal, family and marriage guidance and psychological and other aspects of health support. However, the college will need to know what expert agencies there are and at what point referrals need to be made.

Many college have been involved in developing highly effective and mutually beneficial inter-agency networks which can:

> Offer mutual support and consultation leading to improved information flow and communication.
>
> Facilitate information collection and dissemination, ultimately leading to improved guidance, referral and access.
>
> Encourage advocacy on behalf of the client group as well as pressure group activities, with a view to prompting new developments in services and provision.
>
> Increase co-ordination and co-operation, thus avoiding wasteful duplication of effort on behalf of the clients and ensuring greater sharing of skills, expertise and resources.
>
> (*Anxious to Work*, FEU, 1987)

In some areas of the country TECs have become actively involved in supporting the development of area guidance networks and have recognised their importance as information, referral and advocacy channels in making education and training more responsive to community needs.

Colleges have also become increasingly aware of the need to help remove some of the more obvious barriers to access and have made positive moves to increase the participation of those adults:

- with young and elderly dependants to care for
- living in rural areas isolated by lack of transport
- with disabilities
- with learning difficulties.

Childcare

Provision of good, reliable and affordable childcare is a key issue in the development of education and training for unemployed adults. Many colleges have established creches, nurseries or arrangements with voluntary childcare agencies, private workplace nurseries and their local social services departments. The need for after-school and holiday childcare is also being addressed, as in many situations pre-school childcare is less of a concern for parents than care for the 'over 5s', both before and after school.

A number of TECs are also encouraging the development of childcare facilities for those participating in Adult Training Programmes. Usually, where this occurs single parents are offered a childcare allowance to enable them to take up trainee or employee status training. Some TECs are also using their Local Initiative Fund and Employment Action Programme to develop community childcare facilities and in certain rural areas mobile creches are being introduced.

Transport

In some areas TECs and local authorities offer financial support for travel costs, but transport availability and cost can be a major barrier to access.

Some colleges have attempted to overcome this barrier by:

- scheduling learning activities to take account of the availability of transport
- providing learning opportunities on an outreach basis, especially in areas with high unemployment
- providing travel vouchers (LA, TEC or ESF funded)
- providing a mini-bus service (LA, TEC or ESF funded).

Support for People with Disabilities

A prime purpose of college activity should be to assist people with disabilities and special needs to become personally and economically independent. This can best be achieved by developing programmes which maximise individual potential, develop self-advocacy skills, encourage ways of overcoming disability and increase mobility, self-reliance and independence. However, in order for this to take place colleges will need to:

- locate learning opportunities on the ground floor
- adapt workshops and equipment
- install specially-designed washrooms and toilets
- improve access to the building with ramps
- ensure that parking places near to the building are available.

Support for Ethnic Minorities

Many people from ethnically diverse backgrounds may feel unable to cross a college threshold because of language and cultural barriers. This barrier is being tackled by those colleges which have prioritised the need to:

- ensure that minority groups' interests are represented on governing boards
- ensure that planning processes and procedures take account of local minority communities and their views
- invest in appropriate bi-lingual marketing approaches to encourage people from different cultures to participate in learning opportunities on or off the college site
- translate all college publicity and programme information into appropriate languages with positive images of black people and a statement emphasising that the college welcomes applications from adults from ethnically diverse backgrounds
- develop recruitment practice to appoint bi-lingual or multi-lingual guidance, support and academic staff
- develop appropriate childcare, social and restaurant facilities.

LEARNING SUPPORT

Once an adult has made the commitment to become a learner, ongoing support becomes even more crucial to the quality of the learning programme. Research has established that most unemployed learners tend to use the course tutor as the main source of help and advice while they are in the college. Specialist advice and guidance which are not an integrated part of the course may not be used by the majority of unemployed learners, a point which needs to be considered when planning both the provision and related staff development.

Many colleges are developing course review systems, action planning and recording of achievement as an integral and automatic aspect of all learning opportunities in encouraging the learner to be in control of the learning experience. The use of APLA techniques is increasingly helping adult learners to start training courses and educational programmes at the most appropriate point, and, as a consequence, reduced drop-out, higher levels of achievement and increased progression to higher levels of further education are being recorded. This increase in motivation and attainment can largely be attributed to an increased empowerment of the learners, who have more control of their learning and involvement in the recording of progress and achievement.

Some colleges have refined this aspect of learning support by involving expert systems and SWIPE cards to guide students and record their progress through appropriate learning programmes. Others extend the use of the Action Plan as an underpinning element of the guidance and review service, and relate it to Records of Achievement. To complement this activity a number of TECs are developing and promoting similar review and recording systems, particularly with reference to the use and effectiveness of Training Credits for unemployed adult learners.

Other aspects of learning support offered by colleges to help unemployed people to make the move into a formal learning environment include:

Compensatory basic skills for those who missed out on compulsory schooling

'Study skills' or 'return to learn' provision

Programmes to develop self-advocacy skills, particularly for those with disabilities

The development of induction courses and taster courses

The development of 'job-searching' skills

Arrangements to accredit advanced qualifications acquired in other countries

ESOL/ABE courses linked with practical skill training and with progression routes to mainstream employment-related courses

> Targeted access provision for certain groups: women, black people, older age-groups, etc.

> Specialist provision such as lip-reading, signing, braille and mobility training.

All other aspects of learner support should be an automatic and integral aspect of provision designed for unemployed adults and should be recognised as being of equal status and value to the actual content and delivery of the training programme. Indeed it may be that an APLA process could actually replace a formal training opportunity. Colleges need to cost these services and recognise this support as a value-added aspect of their provision.

The Unemployed Learner's Perspective

Pre-Entry:
Deciding to participate

On the basis of publicity, word of mouth or advice from an external advice or guidance agency, an internal college counsellor or Client Services/Student Services Unit, the unemployed adult decides to participate:

(a) through a TEC funded Adult Training Programme (trainee or employee status)

(b) as a self-referral to participate in college activity (probably under 21 hours so that benefits are not affected, perhaps with fee concessions)

(c) as a trainee on a European Social Fund supported course or through other forms of sponsorship.

At Entry:
Responding to the learner's needs

Arrange a mutually convenient meeting to:

(a) assess prior learning experiences and achievements

(b) offer initial guidance regarding an appropriate programme of learning tailored to meet the individual learner's needs, bearing in mind the context of the referral

(c) assist and negotiate with the learner the drawing up of an action plan focusing on:

- what is to be learned and how it is to be learned
- what is to be assessed, how and when it is to be assessed
- how the learning process is to be accredited and evaluated

(d) agree the action plan with other parties if applicable, e.g. employer, training manager, work placement officer, etc.

(e) invite the client to an induction welcoming session which will provide:

- practical information on what support the college can offer, such as childcare, transport, top-up basic skills, study skills, etc.

  - an introductory tour of the college and the services it can offer
  - an option to join a programme of sessions on study skills, tasters, IT, basic skills, CV construction, etc.

During the Learning Programme:
Supporting the learner

On the basis of the negotiated action plan, the learner then embarks upon an individual learning programme having at all times access to appropriate support, including on-demand:

- assessment of learning and achievement
- advice and guidance
- reassessment of needs
- recording of achievement and progress
- revision and renegotiation of Action Plan
- refocusing of personal and sponsor's targets.

In this way the individual learning programme becomes a means of empowering both the learner and the tutors involved by enhancing the learner's abilities and competences in moving towards 'self-actualisation' (the highest order in Maslow's hierarchy of needs).

At the End

By encouraging the process of 'empowerment' in order to identify and provide individual vocational, educational and life experiences it could be argued that there will always be new learning needs, and that there should never be an end as such – hence the argument and rationale for 'life-long learning'. In practical terms, however, particularly if the unemployed learner was funded by a sponsoring agency, the end becomes more of a measurable reality, whether in terms of NVQ level II, full-time employment, a job-share opportunity or a place on an Access to HE course.

Historically, colleges have found it difficult to record the outcomes, destinations and progression routes of learners, but, increasingly, this kind of information is being recorded on the college management information system. Clients are tracked and in many cases offered an after-care service. The extent to which client tracking or after-care is taken up will largely depend upon the co-operation of the clients, but early evidence suggests that this offer of support, not always directly related to the take-up of additional training, can have long-term benefits for the college in terms of being seen as a caring and responsive organisation in the eyes of the community it serves. It is also an effective way of promoting learning as an ongoing, life-long process.

Case Study: Developing Learner Support at Walsall College of Technology

In 1989 Walsall College agreed a mission statement which showed a commitment to values which were designed to remove impediments to learning and provide a quality learning framework for over 7,000 part-time students and 1,000-plus full-time students.

This commitment resulted in *Student Focus*, the key features which were:

A Student Services team – of eight multi-cultural counsellors, a Youth and Community worker, a Careers Adviser and associated administrative staff.

Student Services Unit – in the converted old college Assembly Hall, with carpeted interview rooms, informal seating and a play area for children.

Accreditation Centre – for APLA and diagnostic skills testing.

Central Admissions Service – counselling and guidance before interviews with admission tutors.

Summer support – during the summer, in conjunction with the Careers Service, post-course and pre-course guidance, counselling and assessment is offered.

Personal Tutor Support – for all learners.

Orientation – a programme of induction for all full-time and part-time students, which includes a pre-course pack as well as planned information/guidance sessions.

The Current Student Journey at Walsall College of Technology

Student Needs	College Response
Pre-entry	
What does the College offer to suit my needs?	Clear, accurate, accessible information on all courses/programmes
Can I find out more without difficulty and without committing myself?	Easy access to trained, well informed Central Admissions specialist staff
Will the College help me to sort out an appropriate programme?	Access to Accreditation Centre, APL, ROA, Learning Agreement
Will the College help me to sort out obstacles before I start (e.g. finance, child care)?	Access to Student Services
At entry and during the programme	
Will I get help in settling in?	Six-weekly review of progress and attendance by Student Focus Teams
What will happen if I am not happy with my programme?	Opportunities to re-negotiate programme with Tutor. Support from Counsellor, Central Admissions
What will happen if I cannot cope with the College?	Tutorial curriculum, study skills, Learning Centre, Tutor/Counsellor
What will happen if I have personal difficulties?	Personal support – Tutor/Counsellor
If I miss classes, will I have to leave?	Above support systems in place
What will happen if I do leave before I complete my programme?	Live student records/ROA portfolio turned into summative document. Tutor/Counselling advice, access to Counselling/careers guidance
Where will I go when I complete my programme?	Exit programmes, careers guidance, advice Tutor/Counsellor
After the learning programme	
Can I still get help even after I have left?	Summer support, continued access to a range of student services

Wendy Morgan, Director of Counselling and Central Admissions, Walsall College of Technology.

ASSESSMENT AND ACCREDITATION

Experience and evidence suggest that most unemployed people are keen to receive some credit for their learning experiences and achievements, and are, more than most people, aware of the increasing pressure of external demands for evidence of achievement, whether in the form of a qualification, portfolio or profile. What should be emphasised, however, is that the assessment and accreditation procedures and methods used should help to promote the benefits of learning and boost morale, rather than become yet another barrier to achievement, and it is for this reason that assessment and accreditation processes should:

- be understood and valued by the learners themselves
- have national currency
- enable learners to build up, record and 'transfer' credit on a cumulative basis
- build on past experience and prior achievement both in and out of unpaid work
- provide a clear picture of progress, achievement or potential
- be competence-based
- enable unemployed people's current skills to be related to training opportunities leading to new occupational skills.

As a result, colleges will need to adapt their standard entry procedures to courses, move away from prescribed prior levels of attainment, certification and formal interview arrangements, and develop more of the learner-focused, 'non-standard entry' arrangements offered by a diverse range of assessment methods and new styles of accreditation.

Government- or TEC-sponsored training has become almost exclusively geared towards provision leading to National Vocational Qualifications (NVQs). NVQs are competence-based and constituted from a number of units, which can be accumulated over time by a variety of routes, whether in the home, class or lecture room, workplace or a simulated working environment. The advantage of the NVQ framework for unemployed adults is that it has the potential to encourage access and progression on the learner's terms rather than on the terms of the awarding body or provider.

The Purpose of Assessment

All learners, regardless of employment status, need assessment to support and develop their learning, and as a way of formally measuring and recognising that they have met specified standards. Assessment should be seen as a positive process that occurs throughout a learning experience, and should help both the learner and the facilitator to identify appropriate education and training routes and reinforce achievement.

Output-related funding is partly based on the achievement of NVQ targets, and where NVQs exist, providers of TEC-sponsored training programmes are normally required to offer them to trainees.

In some occupational sectors there may be little choice, but in others, such as retail and business, there may be a range of NVQs at any given level. These may be equivalent in level, but may differ in cost, administrative procedures and assessment methods.

In selecting which NVQ to offer to an unemployed learner, particular assessment techniques and processes will also need to be chosen, and this will obviously affect the length and cost of the training programme.

Types of Assessment

In *New Approaches to Adult Training* (NIACE/TEED, 1990) the following types of assessment are noted:

1. Traditional Norm-referenced assessment (e.g. GCSEs, 'A' level): ranks individual performance by comparing it with that of others taking the same course level of education and training. It becomes less appropriate with adult learners, as it takes no notice of the different starting points of learners, of prior achievement or of experience, and therefore could disadvantage an unemployed person or returner to work.

2. Criterion-referenced assessment: specifies the amount of learning that has to be achieved and the minimum standards required. It relies on a range of evidence such as pass/fail, competent/not yet competent rather than precise measurements of achievement. It encourages motivation and may boost confidence, but does not provide an indication of ranked performance.

3. Personally-referenced assessment: measures individual progress towards pre-determined standards in relation to individual starting points. It is an integral aspect of personal action planning and competence-based credit accumulation schemes. The adult learner would be involved in a process of self-assessment and measurement of progress in building a personal portfolio and record of achievement.

4. Assessment of Prior Learning and Achievement (APLA): the growth of unit-based assessment of competence through NVQs has led to a recognition that it is desirable to assess individuals' existing competences before designing specific training programmes for them. There are two advantages to this:
   - motivation is increased by giving value to existing competences
   - training costs and duration can be reduced by focusing on individual priority needs or skills deficits.

   APLA can be an integral part of initial assessment, and where it is also used as a diagnostic process it could help guide a learner towards the most appropriate vocational qualifications or learning support. It can also be used, with the collection of appropriate evidence, in giving credit towards units of a qualification.

   As an assessment option for adults returning to training, the advantages of APLA cannot be denied, but the process is expensive in terms of time and requires experienced and accredited staff. However, where colleges have successfully included APLA as one option of assessment and as a tool of flexible learning, the levels of client achievement, satisfaction and retention rates have increased. Moreover, the skills of the assessors have been in great demand, and have been 'bought in' by employers and other training providers.

Some colleges have developed learning, guidance and assessment centres which provide assessment on demand for the college and outside clients.

The APLA process does not only refer to evidence gathered in the workplace or work situation, it can also be based on unpaid work, a particularly significant development for colleges providing opportunities for women and other returners to work.

5. Workplace Assessment: One of the most important sources of evidence for assessment purposes is performance in the workplace, and some NVQs can be gained almost entirely in the work situation. Unless an unemployed person is on a training programme with a work placement, then this kind of assessment is inappropriate. However, many colleges have developed simulated work environments, such as hairdressing salons, restaurants, retail businesses, nurseries, office services, etc. which enable learners without employment to have their performance in a working environment assessed.

Training for assessing, both by the staff of a simulated as well as a work-based training programme, is essential, and NCVQ has recognised that competent assessors and verifiers are one of the most obvious requirements for ensuring effective implementation of NVQs and SVQs. Colleges may also need advice on how to set up effective workplace simulations and how to devise appropriate and cost-effective workplace assessment. This point is reinforced by the fact that a number of organisations and colleges have already prepared information and resource packs in order to share their experience with others.

National Standards for Assessment and Verification

As progress accelerates towards completion of the NVQ framework attention is increasingly focusing on the formation of NVQs and SVQs which demand new and more flexible forms of assessment.

The Training and Development Lead Body has produced the required units of competence for assessment and verification, and it is anticipated that the national standards in assessment awarded by one body will be recognised by others.

The units represent distinctive roles:

1. Assess Candidate Performance: This is designed for the 'Front Line Assessor', the college tutor, the workshop trainer or workplace supervisor. The main assessment skills required are:

   - observation of performance
   - judgement of the performance outcomes
   - determination of underpinning knowledge and understanding.

2. Assess Candidate using Diverse Evidence: This is designed for the 'Second-line Assessor', who will need to draw on a wide range of evidence in making assessment decisions, The main assessment skills required are:

   - observation and judgement of a wide range of sources of evidence, for example: client and peer reports, prior achievement, judgements made by other assessors.

3. **Co-ordinate the Assessment Process:** This is designed for the 'internal verifier' in assessing quality in assessment arrangements in an approved assessment centre, such as a college. The main skills required are:

- assessor support, advice and information
- co-ordinating the collection of evidence
- the internal verification of assessment practice.

It is anticipated that colleges will need a number of internal verifiers to represent the range of qualifications on offer.

4. **Verify the Assessment Process:** This is designed for the 'external verifier', who is normally employed by the awarding body concerned, and who will advise and liaise with the college verifiers.

5. **Identify Previously Acquired Competence:** This is designed for the staff involved in helping clients to put forward competence claims and evidence as part of 'Accreditation of Prior Learning/Achievement' and would naturally link with Unit D32.

Implications for Colleges

Early evidence suggests that TECs and other sponsors of training may well request that providers of assessment or training programmes offer qualified and competent assessors and verifiers, in ensuring both quality and credible national standards.

Credit Accumulation and Recording of Achievement

One of the major barriers to access and progression for adults returning to learning has been the lack of mutual recognition for qualifications. NCVQ and the awarding bodies are at last attempting to break down this particular artificial barrier by creating a framework for credit accumulation and transfer between different occupational sectors and training programmes. The main advantage of this for unemployed adults is that they need not complete their accumulation of credits in one continuous period of study, therefore accommodating employment opportunities when they arise, without losing any credit towards learning. This structure is well developed by the higher education sector, through the CNAA framework for CATS (Credit Accumulation and Transfer Scheme) which enables HE institutions to award credit for achievement in participating colleges and other centres.

Similarly, where a college belongs to an Open College Network a system of credit accumulation and transfer can also exist to enable learners to progress through a variety of vocational and non-vocational, informal and formal learning opportunities. Records of Achievement or 'Passports to Learning' can help in this process of credit accumulation. For many unemployed people the National Record of Vocational Achievement (NROVA) has been of tremendous value in recording not only NVQ units but also evidence of prior achievement and experience in paid and unpaid work.

The flexibility inherent in credit accumulation systems particularly benefits unemployed learners in enabling them to:

- enter and re-enter training programmes outside conventional course times/enrolment periods

- build upon past and often fragmented learning experiences
- have non-college based experiential or work-based learning recognised and accredited
- take a more proactive role in agreeing and managing their own learning plan
- identify gaps in knowledge or skills to participate in short enhancement programmes in order to progress to higher level or professional training
- invest in their training during times of unemployment or part-time employment, and take advantage of short-term contract or job opportunities when they arise (an increasingly common employment practice).

Employment and Work Progression

In providing learning opportunities for unemployed adults, colleges should also demonstrate their ability and commitment to help facilitate the transition from education and training to employment. This can be provided at all stages of a learning programme and should focus on:

- giving more information to employers and clients on the advantages of new, more flexible accreditation processes
- making use of computerised systems such as NCVQ or TAP databases
- effective liaison and collaboration with job market agencies, the TECs and employers
- appropriate and relevant learning opportunities in relation to realistic work opportunities and local employer requirements
- effective vocational guidance provisions
- the development of bridging, orientation and induction courses with local employers
- the development of customised training or adult compacts
- the integral development of job search skills and job retention skills as part of all learning programmes.

A number of colleges offer this kind of service to all learners regardless of employment status as part of their commitment to learner support, and it should certainly be seen as an essential element of all education and training for unemployed adults.

Personal and Educational Progression

Progression should also be an entitlement that all provision for the unemployed offers over and above the opportunity to enhance and improve employment prospects and should be an integral aspect of the action planning/recording of achievement process.

The following indicators of progression demonstrate ways in which unwaged adults can move forward as a consequence of their learning experience:

- achievement of qualifications
- increased knowledge and competence
- development of positive attitudes and motivation
- increased personal confidence and optimism
- changed life directions and sense of purpose.

The challenge and opportunity for colleges is to value these indicators of success, and, as part of the overall marketing strategy, promote and budget for their value-added quality as part of encouraging life-long learning.

AFTER-CARE

Several public and service sector industries have developed after-care services in demonstrating their commitment to quality and client-centredness. Colleges may also wish to emphasise their customer service orientation by including as part of a priced training package a six-month or year-long 'educational service guarantee' which should entitle an unemployed learner or sponsoring agency to:

- advice and guidance on further learning opportunities in and out of the college
- an ongoing action-planning service which will assess and monitor new skills, experience and knowledge
- learner peer group support (e.g. 'The UB40 Network')
- favourable or reduced fees for re-enrolment, training check-ups or updating of records of achievement.

section 5 OPERATIONAL MANAGEMENT

Organising and resourcing provision

Staffing

Human resource development

Accommodation

Administration

Quality assurance

Section 5
OPERATIONAL MANAGEMENT

The Challenge

The challenge of operating as a flexible, learner-centred organisation in widening access to unemployed adults implies that colleges will need to:

- identify and deploy resources both human and physical, in such a way that encourages the development of flexible approaches to learning, assessment and accreditation
- consider new sources of funding and new approaches to the internal costing, pricing and development of resources
- reconsider staff roles and functions and retain or recruit as appropriate
- adapt buildings in order to provide for new services and styles of learning
- develop appropriate performance indicators for evaluating the effectiveness of both the learning process and learner-centred services
- establish appropriate management information and administrative systems to support both learner and manager.

ORGANISING AND RESOURCING PROVISION

Negative feedback on college provision for unemployed adults by both clients and sponsors of training tends to focus on:

> The inflexibility of responding to requests for training opportunities. Unemployment does not happen at one time of year, that is *'when September enrolment takes place'*; and *'unemployed people have a diverse range of experience and skills, not just basic skills'*.

> The difficulty of getting information and advice about college provision, or *'it's difficult to track down the right contact'*.

> The length, duration and timing of provision: *'even though I may still be unemployed, it's hard to commit myself to a year-long course'*; *'if I do more than 21 hours study at college, I lose my benefits'*; *'I can't come along to a 9 o'clock lecture because I have to drop my daughter off at school'*.

> The image of the college: *'I thought it was just for young people'*;
> *'it seems very intimidating and off-putting'*.

Yet, in most cases, these are stereotypical impressions, and often ill-founded. Most colleges are working towards removing these barriers to learning and are doing so through major organisational change, change which is often as much to do with attitude as restructuring or rebuilding.

Colleges which have achieved success and a strong reputation for providing quality education and training for unemployed adults highlight some of the following operational and organisational features:

- there should be a named person and/or contact number available at least during normal college hours
- a staffed client services unit, at ground level, with welcoming reception area, private interview rooms, open all year round
- a cross-college team of appointed 'agents' for unemployed clients, preferably in each major SOC area
- an employer liaison service for arranging placements, work-based assessment and work-experience
- an unemployment issues adviser and local inter-agency guidance network co-ordinator or representative
- an information database on the local labour market and training opportunities
- a team of APLA assessors and outreach work-based assessors to ensure that learners start at the most appropriate level
- a resource-based learning centre to encourage more flexible approaches to participation
- multi-skills workshops in a range of occupational and generic skills areas
- simulated work environments (offices, shops, restaurant, beauty-salon, nursery, employment agency, etc.) to support work-based assessment
- workshops for basic skills, job search activities and language development
- appropriately trained guidance workers who are multilingual where appropriate
- access and learning support for people with disabilities and learning difficulties
- a lounge or study area appropriate for adult learners from a range of cultures and backgrounds
- childcare facilities, college creche or arrangements with private day nursery
- involvement of all appropriate staff in decision-making and planning processes.

Essentially, the key organisational and resourcing issues are:

- a flatter organisational structure to encourage more effective communication and cross-college functions
- the recruitment and development of new hybrid organisers of learning who are neither conventional lecturer nor administrator
- adaptation or development of the college to provide a more adult-centred learning environment, with both learner and learning support services.

Resource Implications

Alternative Internal Budgeting

Considering alternative approaches to the internal budgeting and resourcing of provision which will take into account the significance and value of learner support services, which play such a key role in the programmes planned with unemployed people, rather than being constrained by the current system based on mode of delivery and attendance. For example:

Wirral Metropolitan College has suggested an approach that allocates resources on the basis of target numbers of unit credits achieved by learners. Resources are adjusted quarterly to encourage flexibility in recruitment and encourage progression. It is then also possible to offset units which are expensive to deliver against units which are cheap to deliver, and to take account of the needs of learners who need a greater or lesser degree of support.

Retraining and Consultancy

A number of colleges are developing short retraining courses and consultancy services, such as those promoted by PICKUP and, in many cases, the excess income generated is invested in priority developments for the college, such as provision for women returners, redundancy counselling and special training needs for adults.

Customised Learning

Some colleges have identified the benefits of working strategically with local employers, whereby customised training or adult compact arrangements are planned and provided to meet the employers' upskilling and backfilling requirements. In this way the total package is agreed on the basis of upgrading the skills of existing employees and training unemployed people to meet the skills gaps. This approach may become even more significant with the increase of companies becoming involved in the 'Investors in People' campaign, which promotes the value of human resource development in increasing the viability of the company.

European Funding

External funding from Europe, largely under 'objectives 4 and 2 in Integrated Development Operational Programmes' has also proved to be a useful source of pump-priming in providing for the unemployed; and, more recently, special programmes have been introduced to encourage greater access to training for women wishing to return to the labour market (NOW and EUROFORM) and for people with special training needs, learning difficulties or the long-term unemployed (HORIZON). Additional emphasis has been placed on the role of adult guidance, and Articles 1 and 1.2 of the second Council regulation (19 December 1988) cover the following:

- Article 1.1 – Support for vocational guidance and counselling built into course submissions.
- Article 1.2 – Support for a free standing service for unemployed adults.

Government Funding

External funding from various government departments has also proved beneficial, particularly that from the Department of Employment, through, for example, the National Development projects – usually planned in conjunction with local TECs.

TEC Support

TECs have also played an increasingly significant role in the funding of research or provision for the adult unemployed. A recent FEU survey (August 1991) which investigated the degree to which TECs contract with colleges for work with the unemployed reported very high numbers. Most TECs reflect their own resourcing arrangements in funding provision based on outputs, such as 'jobs', further education or training, NVQs and self-employment. Some TECs say they are looking at more imaginative and equitable approaches related to client performance rather than output alone. Undoubtedly the colleges have an influential role to play in this collaborative area of work.

The impact of ERA is only just beginning to make an impression on the ways in which colleges resource, cost and budget provision. It seems likely that the new legislation post April 1993 will again considerably influence the ways in which colleges can plan and provide for their unemployed clients.

STAFFING

All the issues and action suggested in this manual have implications for the skills, roles and functions of college staff. The emphasis on learner-centred approaches presupposes that staff accustomed to formal traditional teaching and lecturing methods will need to develop a more flexible and responsive approach to adult learning styles. This may require the development of:

- initial diagnosis and assessment of existing skills
- assessment of prior achievements and experience both in paid and unpaid work
- guidance and counselling skills
- negotiation of learning objectives and realistic outcomes
- action planning, monitoring and reviewing of progress
- anti-racist and anti-sexist approaches
- outreach and marketing skills
- employer liaison skills
- collection and collation of management information about client outcomes and destinations
- skills to produce or adapt open learning materials
- project-based assessment
- the design and management of simulated work environments
- team teaching or cross-programme teaching
- supervisory, administrative and management skills.

Support staff and administrators may well need to adjust their roles in the light of new responsibilities such as:

- continuous enrolment
- managing and recording information on individual learning plans, contracts or records of achievement
- tracing past clients to record their destinations and levels of satisfaction with the provision
- on-going information and guidance for adult learners as part of their entitlement to learning
- the recording of client information for future planning purposes
- referrals to other providers of training
- managing of resource-based learning workshops.

Increasingly the different roles may overlap and merge as colleges attempt to become more customer-oriented and adult-friendly. This will inevitably have implications for the development of college-wide staff and human resource development strategies.

HUMAN RESOURCE DEVELOPMENT

If staff are to perform competently the new roles expected of them, then a budgeted, college-wide human resource development strategy will be needed. A useful starting point may well be a staff training audit which identifies:

- corporate training needs (such as anti-racist and anti-sexist training, or the nature of adult learners)
- functional training needs (such as marketing, CADCAM updating)
- generic training needs (such as counselling, assessment of prior learning).

A strategy would need to take into account:

- existing staff expertise in adult learning developed in all areas of the college (vocational, non-vocational and administrative). It would need also to encourage those staff to become mentors to less experienced members of staff
- the importance of emphasising the process as well as the content of the staff development programme
- the value of encouraging all staff, whatever level, full or part-time, to take advantage of their entitlement to staff development
- the importance of accrediting or validating the staff development on offer whether on an in-house or national basis.

If the strategy is to have college-wide impact, it may be worth considering the ways in which the Investor In People national standard could be developed within the college, with support from the local TEC.

> **AN INVESTOR IN PEOPLE**
>
> Makes a public commitment from the top to develop all employees to achieve its business objectives.
>
> Regularly reviews the training and development needs of all employees.
>
> Takes action to train and develop individuals on recruitment and throughout their employment.
>
> Evaluates the investment in training and development to assess achievement and improve future effectiveness.
>
> *The National Standard – Links to Assessment Indicators* (1991 ED Ref 11P29).

The actual delivery of the staff development programme will inevitably depend upon the amount of funding available, but relatively cost-effective programmes can be developed on an in-house basis, using existing staff expertise. This could be supported by:

- planning joint ventures with other colleges
- 'shadowing' secondments with the local TEC, employers, voluntary sector organisations, community centres, Employment Services, etc.
- links with regional or local 'adult-focused' networks such as PICKUP and NVQ development agents, Open College Networks, Guidance and Community Education networks, etc.
- 'buying in' a consultant with expertise in an under-developed skill, e.g. APLA.

Whatever the approach, it is essential that human resource development is recognised as a priority activity in changing the college culture to best meet the diverse learning needs of unemployed adults.

ACCOMMODATION

With an emphasis on flexibility of delivery, on resource based learning and the importance of guidance and learner support, it is inevitable that traditional lecture-halls, classroom and workshops will have to be modified or adapted to cater for these new delivery styles and client groups. In many cases the changes can be made fairly easily, for example in some colleges:

- ground-floor administration and management suites have been changed into welcoming reception areas with client services and learner support services taking precedence over other functions
- lecture theatres or halls have been converted into open plan, resource-based learning workshops, creches and guidance assessment centres, simulated work environments, adult-only study, lounge or workshop areas
- unused caretakers' houses have become independent guidance units, day-nurseries, employment agencies and enterprise support units

- libraries have become resource-based learning centres, with access to video, tape, fax, photocopying and computing facilities
- traditional classrooms and workshops have been transformed by the addition of carpets, curtains, less formal seating arrangements and potted plants.

Some of the conversion work has been carried out as in-house, project-based training. Some colleges have held fund-raising events or raffles to raise money, others have turned to industry for their support. For example, computer hardware and business technology companies have often seen this kind of support as financially beneficial in the long-term.

Some colleges have made more radical and resource-intensive changes by investing in:

- town-centre or high street venues for adult guidance, assessment and training, recognising the inaccessibility (psychologically and physically) of their main site
- mobile information and learning units, which can be driven to the more remote areas of a college's catchment area
- the hire of hotels, Unemployed Workers' Centres or community centre rooms, which may be more appropriate for the delivery of certain types of learning opportunities for unemployed adults
- the purchase of restaurants, pubs, factories, shops, offices, and hotels to develop the increasing demand for work-based training and competences in the workplace, particularly in areas where 'employer-placements' are increasingly difficult to find.

Evidence suggests that most colleges have already modified or intend to modify their buildings to make them more accessible for people with disabilities or sensory impairments, for example:

- installation of specially-designed toilets and washing facilities
- ground-floor learning centres and study areas
- provision of lifts, ramps and wide doors
- special parking spaces near the college entrance
- adaptation of workshops and equipment.

Most colleges recognise the importance of improving the quality, suitability and appearance of their accommodation, and regard the short-term costs as a long-term investment in the future effectiveness of their service to the community.

ADMINISTRATION

A key challenge for any manager of learning is to ensure that there is no conflict between flexibility and efficiency. This conflict management depends on highly effective management information and administrative systems that will provide a helpful service to learners and their sponsors, and at the same time support the management of flexible access to learning, assessment and accreditation.

Many colleges are addressing these issues through the introduction of:

- inter-college meetings which involve administrative staff at all stages of development planning
- all-year round enrolment and college orientation procedure
- understandable, multi-lingual information on fees, fee remissions and eligibility criteria
- enrolment forms which become the basis of records of achievement and/or action plans
- flexible fee structures and methods of payment, such as 'pay as you learn' schemes, purchase of training vouchers, fees based on 'learning hours' or units of training
- computerised systems of registration, such as SWIPE cards, which learners use on entering and leaving a workshop or learning centre. Most of the software packages act not only as registers, but record learner details, achievements and outcomes. The information can be used to monitor progress and destinations and follow-up 'drop-out'
- specific fee packages for non-teaching provision such as guidance, counselling, APLA, action planning, initial assessment and diagnosis. The fees will be based on 'notional' staff time rather than actual time, on the grounds that some learners may be 'fast-trackers' and others may require more support
- referral systems and databases which will support learners in their search for more appropriate training, advanced education, a job, self-employment, personal guidance, financial advice, etc.
- computerised management information systems (CMIS) that can be readily updated and interpreted, so that information on achievements and destination is available to both sponsors of training and college planning teams.

Initially these changes will have implications for staff development and provide a useful opportunity for planning joint events or courses for teaching and non-teaching members of the college.

QUALITY ASSURANCE

The essential stages in any review of performance are:

- the establishment of clear objectives and goals
- the monitoring of progress in achieving these objectives through indicators of success, and achievement of targets and milestones
- taking action to improve progress and set new objectives in assuring managing quality.

In recent years, colleges have been expected to develop and use performance indicators that measure their efficiency and effectiveness according to nationally laid-down criteria such as:

- course costs per FTE client
- qualification rate and costs per FTE
- completion rate/costs per FTE
- progression/placement rate per FTE

- non-teacher costs per FTE
- staff/student ratio
- average class size.

The problem of using these criteria is that they have been designed in relation to resource allocation and tend to focus on financial outputs based on traditional full-time, year-long courses. Colleges wishing to plan, provide and deliver more learner-focused, flexible learning opportunities may well find these measures unrealistic and irrelevant.

The conventional measures of learning success, examination passes and qualifications, are not relevant to all unemployed learners, particularly those sponsored by TECs, who may require competence-based or unit-based programmes which assess learning success in terms of modules or specific skills acquisition. Similarly, the use of completion-rates may be misleading as an indicator of 'educational success', as drop-out is usually due to non-educational reasons such as finding a job, domestic commitments, financial or health problems. Whatever criteria are established, the quantitative measures must be supplemented by qualitative feedback from the clients and sponsors, and should be collected and recorded from the moment a client or prospective client comes into contact with the college.

To date most TECs are using ATO criteria in contracting arrangements with training providers, although the FEU/REPLAN survey (August 1991) revealed that over half the TECs were working towards their own local quality standards, and 15% were considering the BS5750 standard as a possible way forward.

Whatever external approach is used it is important that internal college quality control and evaluation mechanisms are developed and understood by all staff working with the unemployed. Effective programme review should include:

Cross-college programme review teams including teaching and non-teaching staff, clients, sponsors and referral agencies such as Employment Services and Guidance Services.

Mechanisms for recording and making use of client and sponsor feedback at the start, during and at the end of a learning programme.

Longitudinal tracking of clients after a learning programme has ended.

Mechanisms for ensuring that equal opportunities targets are being achieved.

Mechanisms for ensuring that health and safety regulations are being monitored and adhered to.

Processes for monitoring and evaluating non-course based activities such as outreach, advice and guidance, assessment, the accreditation of prior achievement, etc.

Methods of reviewing the effectiveness of different promotional and publicity activities.

A variety of data collection methods including interviews, reports, questionnaires, group discussion, etc.

Mechanisms for 'feeding back' and influencing the strategic planning processes of the college and others such as the TEC or LEC, or local authority.

In *Supporting the Unemployed in FE* (FEU 1988), evaluation was used to identify six key outcomes for unemployed people:

- progression to employment
- progression to new education and training opportunities
- growth in personal effectiveness
- development of vocational skills
- gaining qualifications
- the development of transferable core skills.

The difficulty of monitoring and evaluating provision for adults in terms of such specific outcomes is that:

- individuals have different objectives and starting points and their objectives may change as a result of the learning process
- adult learning has a range of likely outcomes, some of which defy quantification (e.g. increase in confidence) (*Opening Colleges to Adult Learners*, NIACE, 1991).

Some TECs are contracting with training providers on the basis of output-related funding and hard outputs such as:

- employment
- self-employment
- further education or training
- NVQs.

Others are considering 'softer' outputs and developing criteria for performance-related funding, which will link closely with individual action plans. Colleges will monitor the extent to which the individual's aims and objectives have been achieved. This approach may be more appropriate for people with special training needs, learning difficulties and language development needs. It should also ensure a more equitable share of training opportunities for the long-term unemployed.

If identifying performance indicators is seen as an important aspect of planning and managing provision for the adult unemployed, then the following decisions will need to be taken:

- select what information it is necessary to collect
- decide how often to collect it
- decide the criteria against which the improvement is to be judged
- establish how the performance indicators will fit into the decision-making process.

Performance indicators should be seen as signals, not absolute measures, and are there to provide questions rather than answers in improving the quality of provision and decision-making.

APPENDIX 1

THE CONTEXT

National Labour Market Information

APPENDIX 1: THE CONTEXT

NATIONAL LABOUR MARKET INFORMATION
Table 1: Forecast Employment Change by Occupation*, UK

	Employment Change (%) 1989–2000	Average Growth (%) 1989–2000
Managers and Administrators	13	1.1
Professional Occupations	20	1.7
Associated Professional and Technical Occupationss	15	1.3
Clerical and Secretarial Occupations	-2	-0.2
Craft and Related Occupations	-1	-0.1
Personal and Protective Services	12	1.0
Sales Occupations	4	-.3
Plant and Machine Operatives	-8	-0.8
Other Occupations	-3	-0.3
Whole Economy	**4**	**0.4**

Excludes H.M. Forces

Source: Institute for Employment Research, 1990.

Figure 1.

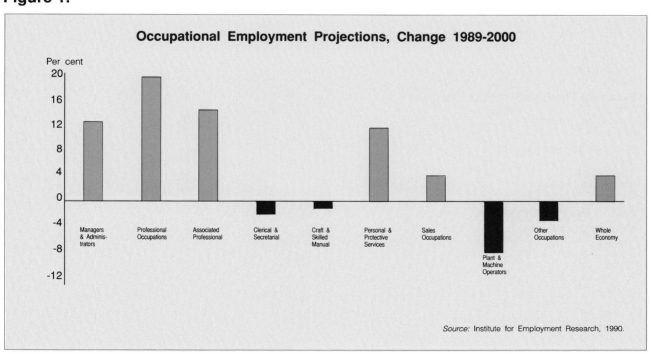

Source: Institute for Employment Research, 1990.

Table 2. Existence and Extent of Recruitment Difficulties by Occupation

	% of all establishments	%* of establishments with recruitment difficulties	% of total hard-to-fill vacancies	% of establishments with difficulties seeking:	
				Qualification.s	Experience
SOC Group					
Managers & Administrators	5	21	18		
Professional Occupations					
of which:		10	10		
Engineers & Technologists		4	2	82	50
Business & Financial Professionals		8	7	81	43
Others					
Associated Professional & Technical Occupations					
of which:					
Computer Analysts/Programmers		4	2	49	78
Scientific Technicians		4	3	93	30
Health Associate Professionals					
Draughtpersons, Quantity & other Surveyors		2	1	79	40
Others		4	2		
Clerical & Sec. Occupations	5	25	15		
of which:					
Secretaries, PAs, Typists, wordprocessing operators		10	7	42	61
Clerks (not elsewhere stated)		4	2	26	52
Numerical clerks & cashiers		3	1	32	58
Others		10	5		
Craft & Related Occupations	5	23	22		
of which:					
Metal Machining, Fitting & Instrument Making		6	3	61	64
Electrical/Electronic Trades		3	3	65	57
Metal Forming, Welding & Related		4	3	43	69
Textiles, Garments & Related Trades		3	6	12	73
Vehicle Trades		4	2	64	52
Others		5	5		
Personal & Protective Service Occupations	2	7	6		
of which:					
Catering Occupations		5	3	39	49
Others		2	2		
Sales Occupations	2	8	7		
of which:					
Sales Assistants		5	4	10	35
Sales Representatives		3	2	16	65
Others		1	-		
Plant & Machine Operatives	2	8	9		
Other Occupations	2	11	7		
of which:					
Other Occupations in Sales & Services		8	5	0	10
Others		3	2		

* Percentage totals greater than 100 percent as establishments could report several types of difficulty

Source: Skill Needs in Britain 1990.

APPENDIX 2

THE EDUCATION AND TRAINING CONTEXT

Appendix 2
THE EDUCATION AND TRAINING CONTEXT

A: A Strategy for Skills (Guidance from the Secretary of State for Employment on Training, Vocational Education and Enterprise, November 1991)

Strategic Priorities for Action

The Government's six priorities for the 1990s are at the centre of the national strategy:

- Employers must invest more effectively in the skills their businesses need.
- Young people must have the motivation to achieve their full potential and to develop the skills the economy needs.
- Individuals must be persuaded that training pays and that they should take more responsibility for their own development.
- People who are unemployed and those at a disadvantage in the jobs market must be helped to get back to work and to develop their abilities to the full.
- The providers of education and training must offer high quality and flexible provision which meets the needs of individuals and employers.
- Enterprise must be encouraged throughout the economy, particularly through the continued growth of small business and self-employment.

B: National Education and Training Targets (A Strategy for Skills)

National education and training targets have been agreed following an initiative launched by the CBI in association with other key partners. The National Training Task Force has agreed to oversee and review progress at national level, and TECs, and local enterprise companies are ideally placed to take the lead locally in achieving the targets.

National Targets *Foundation Learning*	National Targets *Lifetime Learning*
1. Immediate moves to ensure that by 1997 at least 80% of all young people attain NVQ/SVQ Level II or its academic equivalent in their foundation education and training.	1. By 1996, all employees should take part in training or development activities as the norm.
2. All young people who can benefit should be given an entitlement to structured training, work experience or education leading to NVQ/SVQ Level III or its academic equivalent.	2. By 1996, at least half of the employed workforce should be aiming for qualifications or units towards them within the NVQ/SVQ framework, preferably in the context of individual action plans and with support from employers.
3. By the year 2000, at least half of the age group should attain NVQ/SVQ Level III or its academic equivalent as a basis for further progression.	3. By the year 2000, 50% of the employed workforce should be qualified to NVQ/SVQ Level III or its academic equivalent as a minimum.
4. All education and training provision should be structured and designed to develop self-reliance, flexibility and broad competence as well as specific skills.	4. By 1996, at least half of the medium-sized and larger organisations should qualify as Investors in People, assessed by the relevant TEC or LEC.

C: Priority 4 (A Strategy for Skills)

People who are unemployed and those at a disadvantage in the jobs market must be helped to get back to work and to develop their abilities to the full.

Training for people who are long-term unemployed, have special training needs including those relating to a disability, or are at a disadvantage in the jobs market, continues to have an important role in enabling them to make their full contribution to the economy. Meeting the needs of these groups is an essential element of the national training strategy.

TECs have a major part to play by helping unemployed people acquire appropriate skills at all ages and at all levels, from those with special education needs or lower achievements, through those requiring basic language training, to the expanding market for those with higher level skills. To achieve this, TECs will need to arrange flexible and responsive provision which enables individuals to gain access to and progress within occupational training.

Priority must, of course, be given to helping those unemployed people covered by the adult guarantee and aim. Those who have special training needs or are otherwise at a disadvantage must not be overlooked either. Within their existing resources, TECs have considerable flexibility to tailor both Employment Training and Employment Action in ways that meet the differing needs of unemployed people in a cost-effective way.

TECs will want to address the particular needs of people in rural areas and inner cities. Some TECs will be able to benefit from links with the Local Authority City Challenge Teams, and to use their flexibilities to maximise local City Challenge aims. There should also be scope in many areas for working with City Action Teams and Task Forces to develop approaches which meet local needs.

The Employment Service is also a major contributor to meeting the needs of unemployed and disadvantaged people. Close and effective relationships between TECs and the Employment Service are essential if the quality of the help is to be maximised.

Employment Action

- provides the opportunity to maintain the work skills needed locally
- offers temporary work and job finding support, coupled with training in basic and job search skills if required
- allows TECs to offer a range of help to the unemployed to meet different needs
- allows TECs, through projects and placements, to contribute to urban regeneration, growth of enterprise, and local economic and environmental developments.

D: Eligibility Criteria

The Guarantee Group: 18–24-year-olds who have been unemployed more than six but less than 12 months.

The Aim Group: those aged 18–49 who have been unemployed for more than two years and disabled people aged 18–59, irrespective of length of unemployment.

TECs may widen access to training for the unemployed by offering provision to those not covered by the above criteria, for example:

• lone parents in receipt of Income Support for at least 26 weeks, whose youngest child is in statutory full-time education
• returners to the labour market
• unemployed (but not necessarily for six months) people who wish to pursue training in skills shortage occupations and in enterprise
• victims of large-scale redundancies.

[Check with your local TEC operations team for specific criteria over and above the Aim and Guarantee Groups.]

APPENDIX 3

WHO ARE
THE UNEMPLOYED?

Appendix 3
WHO ARE THE UNEMPLOYED?

The Employment Service requirements for the 25-week unemployment qualifying period

Only periods spent in/covered by the following count towards the 26-week unemployment qualifying period:

- signing on with the Employment Service (and regarded by the Employment Service as being available for work during such periods)
- in receipt of Invalidity Benefit, Sickness Benefit or Severe Disablement Allowance
- any number of breaks of up to 14 calendar days' duration, e.g. holidays or short-term work (although regular temporary work with the same employer would constitute a break in unemployment)
- employment with earnings of £2.00 per day or less
- in prison, whether on a custodial sentence or on remand. Where applicants seek entry to Training For Adults after leaving prison and satisfy the 26-week unemployment qualifying period on discharge, there is no requirement for them to sign-on at an Employment Service Local Office before entering the programme
- on voluntary work when entitlement to social security benefits or National Insurance credits is not affected
- on a training course when no training allowance was paid, and the applicant continued to sign on over the period of the course
- temporary disqualification from social security benefit or National Insurance credits
- on public duties, e.g. councillors, JPs, jury service or Territorial Army Service, irrespective of any allowances received
- in part-time employment when unemployment benefit is being claimed for the days on which the individual is not working.

The following periods do not count towards the qualifying weeks:

- a period spent on an allowance-supported rehabilitation course should not be regarded as a break in unemployment, but neither should it count towards the 26–week qualifying period
- time spent on Youth Training should count as a break in unemployment.